Easy Layer-Cake Quilts

SIMPLE QUILTS THAT START WITH 10" SQUARES

BARBARA GROVES AND MARY JACOBSON
of Me and My Sister Designs

Martingale
Create with Confidence

Easy Layer-Cake Quilts: Simple Quilts That Start with
10" Squares
© 2017 by Barbara Groves and Mary Jacobson

Martingale®
19021 120th Ave. NE, Ste. 102
Bothell, WA 98011-9511 USA
ShopMartingale.com

Printed in China
22 21 20 19 18 17   8 7 6 5 4 3 2 1

Library of Congress Cataloging-in-Publication Data
Names: Groves, Barbara, author. | Jacobson, Mary A., author.
Title: Easy layer-cake quilts : simple quilts that start with 10"
     squares / Barbara Groves and Mary Jacobson.
Description: Bothell, WA : Martingale, [2017]
Identifiers: LCCN 2017017666 | ISBN 9781604688658
Subjects: LCSH: Patchwork--Patterns. | Quilting--Patterns.
Classification: LCC TT835 .G7676 2017 | DDC 746.46/041--dc23
LC record available at https://lccn.loc.gov/2017017666

MISSION STATEMENT

We empower makers who use fabric and yarn
to make life more enjoyable.

CREDITS

**PUBLISHER AND
CHIEF VISIONARY OFFICER**
Jennifer Erbe Keltner

CONTENT DIRECTOR
Karen Costello Soltys

DESIGN MANAGER
Adrienne Smitke

MANAGING EDITOR
Tina Cook

PRODUCTION MANAGER
Regina Girard

ACQUISITIONS EDITOR
Karen M. Burns

**COVER AND
INTERIOR DESIGNER**
Kathy Kotomaimoce

TECHNICAL EDITOR
Ellen Pahl

PHOTOGRAPHER
Brent Kane

COPY EDITOR
Melissa Bryan

ILLUSTRATOR
Lisa Lauch

Contents

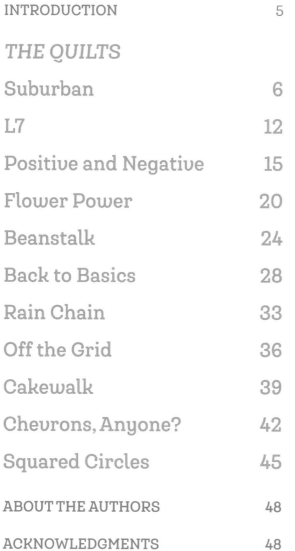

Introduction

Layer Cakes! For us there couldn't be a more fitting name for a fabric precut. After all, it's our favorite dessert in the form of fabric—and it doesn't get much better than that!

So what is a Layer Cake? Layer Cake is a term trademarked by Moda Fabrics to describe a bundle of 42 precut fabric squares that measure 10" × 10". Each Layer Cake usually contains at least one square of each fabric from an entire collection.

This book features 11 projects, each made using Layer Cake precuts. All of the quilts are designed for confident beginners and beyond. None are overly time intensive, and most can be completed in a few days. For best results, be sure to read the "quilt recipes" carefully before cutting.

Let's get baking!

~Barb and Mary

Suburban

Finished quilt: 72" × 72" • Finished block: 8" × 8"

Made with the Good Morning fabric line by Me and My Sister Designs

> You won't need a contractor's license to design this community. Feel free to spruce up your village by quilting fun designs in the spaces between houses. If you look closely, you'll spot a lemonade stand and a doghouse in ours.

Materials

Yardage is based on 42"-wide fabric.

30 squares, 10" × 10", of assorted prints for House blocks*

⅓ yard of white solid for doors and windows

1⅞ yards of blue solid for roof backgrounds and between-block sashing

1 yard of light blue print for between-row sashing and inner border

½ yard of dark blue print for middle border

1 yard of blue floral for outer border

⅝ yard of blue stripe for binding

4½ yards of fabric for backing

80" × 80" piece of batting

A Moda Layer Cake contains 42 squares, 10" × 10". The quilt shown includes 6 green, 3 blue, 2 turquoise, 6 pink, 4 orange, 5 purple, and 4 yellow print squares.

Cutting

All measurements include ¼" seam allowances. Divide the 30 squares into 2 groups: 15 for the houses and 15 for the roofs. Refer to the cutting guides at right when cutting the squares; keep like prints together.

From *each* of the 15 squares for houses, cut:

1 rectangle, 3" × 10" (15 total)

1 rectangle, 4" × 7" (15 total)

1 rectangle, 2" × 4" (15 total)

2 rectangles, 1½" × 2" (30 total)

2 rectangles, 1½" × 2½" (30 total)

From *each* of the 15 squares for roofs, cut:

1 rectangle, 3½" × 8½" (15 total)

1 rectangle, 4½" × 8½" (15 total)

From the white solid, cut:

3 strips, 2½" × 42"; crosscut into 15 rectangles, 2½" × 8"

1 strip, 2" × 42"; crosscut into 15 squares, 2" × 2"

From the blue solid, cut:

3 strips, 3½" × 42"; crosscut into 30 squares, 3½" × 3½"

4 strips, 4½" × 42"; crosscut into 30 squares, 4½" × 4½"

5 strips, 2½" × 42"; crosscut into 20 rectangles, 2½" × 8½"

2 strips, 8½" × 42"; crosscut into:
- 4 rectangles, 8½" × 12½"
- 2 rectangles, 8½" × 10½"

From the light blue print, cut:

8 strips, 2½" × 42"

6 strips, 2" × 42"

From the dark blue print, cut:

7 strips, 2" × 42"

From the blue floral, cut:

7 strips, 4¼" × 42"

From the blue stripe, cut:

8 strips, 2¼" × 42"

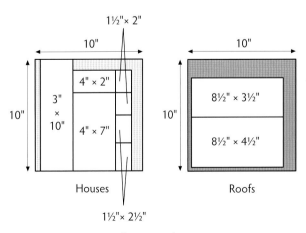

Cutting guides

Making the Block Units

Use a ¼"-wide seam allowance and a small stitch length throughout. Press all seam allowances open, unless otherwise noted.

Each house base will be cut in half to make two different House blocks, one with a pointed roof and one with a flat roof. Choose one print 4½" × 8½" rectangle for the pointed roof and a different print 3½" × 8½" rectangle for the flat roof.

HOUSE BASES

1 Arrange and sew together one white 2" square, two print 1½" × 2" rectangles, one print 2" × 4" rectangle, and one print 4" × 7" rectangle as shown. Make 15 units that measure 4" × 10", including seam allowances.

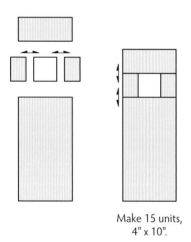

Make 15 units,
4" x 10".

2 Sew one white 2½" × 8" rectangle, two print 1½" × 2½" rectangles, and one print 3" × 10" rectangle together as shown. Make 15 units that measure 5" × 10", including seam allowances.

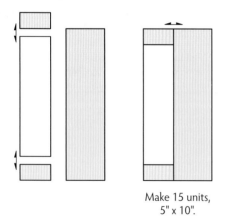

Make 15 units,
5" x 10".

3 Sew the units from steps 1 and 2 together as shown. Make a total of 15 house bases that measure 8½" × 10", including seam allowances.

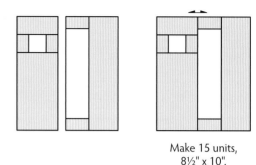

Make 15 units,
8½" x 10".

POINTED ROOFS

For each pointed roof you will need one print 4½" × 8½" rectangle and two blue solid 4½" background squares.

1 Draw a diagonal line from corner to corner on the wrong side of each of the blue solid 4½" squares.

2 With right sides facing, layer a marked blue square on one end of a print 4½" × 8½" rectangle. Stitch on the marked line. Trim the seam allowances to ¼". Flip and press. Layer a second marked square on the opposite end of the rectangle. Stitch, trim, flip, and press as before. Make a total of 15 pointed roof units that measure 4½" × 8½", including seam allowances.

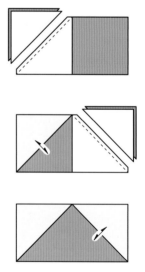

Make 15 units,
4½" x 8½".

FLAT ROOFS

For each flat roof you will need one print 3½" × 8½" rectangle and two blue solid 3½" squares.

1 Draw a diagonal line from corner to corner on the wrong side of each of the blue solid 3½" squares.

2 With right sides facing, layer a marked blue square on one end of a print 3½" × 8½" rectangle. Stitch on the marked line. Trim the seam allowances to ¼". Flip and press. Layer a second marked square on the opposite end of the rectangle. Stitch, trim, flip, and press as before. Make a total of 15 flat roof units that measure 3½" × 8½", including seam allowances.

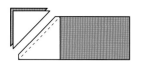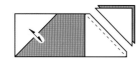

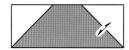

Make 15 units,
3½" x 8½".

Completing the Blocks

1 Arrange and sew together one house base, one coordinating pointed roof, and one coordinating flat roof as shown. The house/roof unit should measure 8½" × 17", including seam allowances. Make 15 units, swapping the placement of the flat and pointed roofs as desired and playing with the fabric groupings to make fun combinations.

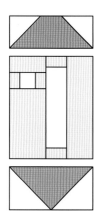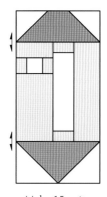

Make 15 units,
8½" × 17".

2 Cut each house/roof unit in half (8½" from one end) as shown to yield two House blocks that measure 8½" square, including seam allowances. Make 30 blocks.

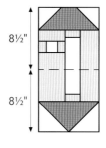

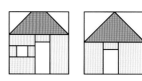

Make 30 blocks,
8½" x 8½".

Assembling the Quilt Top

The quilt top is assembled in horizontal rows; each row contains five houses, but their placement and the number of blue sashing pieces varies from row to row. You may want to lay out all the rows before joining the House blocks, to make sure you like the arrangement of your colors. Each completed row should measure 8½" × 58½", including seam allowances.

1 For row 1, arrange and sew together five House blocks, three blue solid 2½" × 8½" rectangles, and one blue solid 8½" × 12½" rectangle as shown.

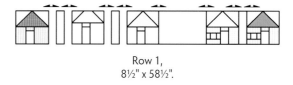

Row 1,
8½" x 58½".

2 For row 2, arrange and sew together five House blocks, four blue solid 2½" × 8½" rectangles, and one blue solid 8½" × 10½" rectangle as shown.

Row 2,
8½" x 58½".

3 For row 3, arrange and sew together five House blocks, three blue solid 2½" × 8½" rectangles, and one blue solid 8½" × 12½" rectangle as shown.

Row 3,
8½" x 58½".

4 For row 4, arrange and sew together five House blocks, four blue solid 2½" × 8½" rectangles, and one blue solid 8½" × 10½" rectangle as shown.

Row 4,
8½" x 58½".

5 For row 5, arrange and sew together five House blocks, three blue solid 2½" × 8½" rectangles, and one blue solid 8½" × 12½" rectangle as shown.

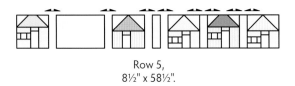

Row 5,
8½" x 58½".

6 For row 6, arrange and sew together five House blocks, three blue solid 2½" × 8½" rectangles, and one blue solid 8½" × 12½" rectangle as shown.

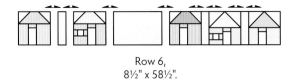

Row 6,
8½" x 58½".

7 Sew the eight light blue 2½" × 42" strips together end to end. From this length, cut five strips, 58½" long, for sashing.

8 Lay out the House rows in order from top to bottom, alternating them with the sashing strips. Sew the rows together and press. The quilt center should measure 58½" square, including seam allowances.

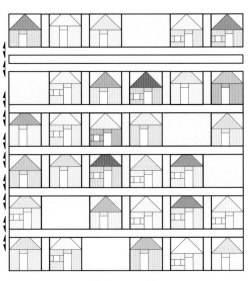

Quilt assembly

Adding Borders

1 For the inner border, piece the six light blue 2" × 42" strips together end to end. From this length, cut two strips, 58½" long, and sew them to the sides of the quilt top.

2 From the remainder of the light blue strip, cut two strips, 61½" long, and sew them to the top and bottom of the quilt top. The quilt top should now measure 61½" square, including seam allowances.

3 For the middle border, piece the seven dark blue 2" × 42" strips together end to end. From this length, cut two strips, 61½" long, and sew them to the sides of the quilt top.

4 From the remainder of the dark blue strip, cut two strips, 64½" long, and sew them to the top and bottom of the quilt top. The quilt top should now measure 64½" square, including seam allowances.

5 For the outer border, piece the seven blue floral 4¼" × 42" strips together end to end. From this length, cut two strips, 64½" long, and sew them to the sides of the quilt top.

6 From the remainder of the blue floral strip, cut two strips, 72" long, and sew them to the top and bottom of the quilt top. The completed quilt top should measure 72" square.

Finishing

If you need more information on any of the finishing steps, go to ShopMartingale.com/HowtoQuilt for free downloadable instructions.

1 Layer the backing, batting, and quilt top; baste the layers together. Hand or machine quilt as desired. Our quilt includes a cloud-like design in the blue background and arcs in the border. Look closely between the houses and you'll see a myriad of detailed designs such as shrubs, trees, fences, a mailbox, and more.

2 Trim and square up the quilt. Make the binding using the blue stripe 2¼"-wide strips and attach it to the quilt.

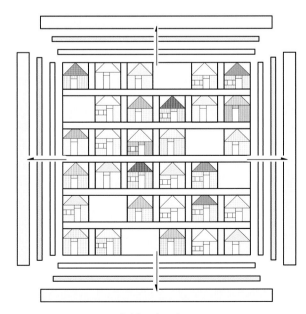

Adding borders

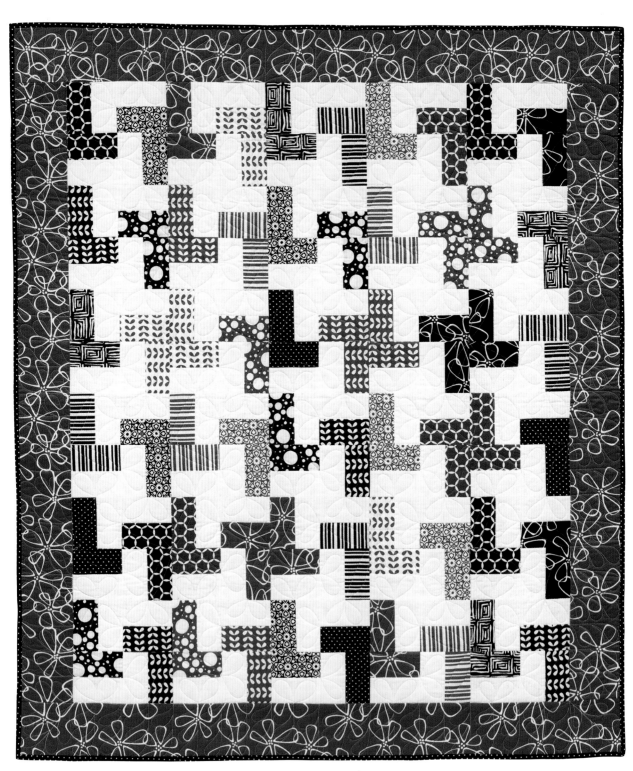

Made with the Shades of Black fabric line by Me and My Sister Designs

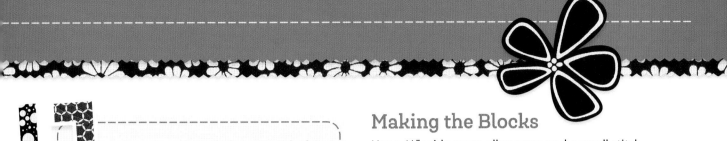

L7

Is it an L or the number 7? With this block, you get both! To spin up even more fun, place blocks of the same fabric side by side to form a pinwheel. Our version is shown in black and gray, but we can easily picture it in vibrant colors. It would be just as fabulous, just as fun, and just as easy!

Materials

Yardage is based on 42"-wide fabric.

15 squares, 10" × 10", of assorted black and gray prints for blocks*
1⅓ yards of white solid for blocks
¾ yard of gray print for border
½ yard of black print for binding
3⅛ yards of fabric for backing
55" × 63" piece of batting

A Moda Layer Cake contains 42 squares, 10" × 10". The quilt shown includes 7 gray print squares and 8 black print squares.

Cutting

All measurements include ¼" seam allowances. Keep like prints together as you cut.

From *each* of the print 10" squares, cut:
4 rectangles, 2½" × 10" (60 total)

From the white solid, cut:
4 strips, 10" × 42"; crosscut into 60 rectangles, 2½" × 10"

From the gray print for border, cut:
5 strips, 4½" × 42"

From the black print for binding, cut:
6 strips, 2¼" × 42"

Making the Blocks

Use a ¼"-wide seam allowance and a small stitch length throughout. Press all seam allowances open, unless otherwise noted.

1 Sew a print 2½" × 10" rectangle to a white 2½" × 10" rectangle to make a strip set as shown. Make four strip sets from each print, for a total of 60.

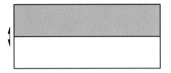

Make 60.

2 Cut each strip set into two 4½"-wide segments. This will yield eight segments, 4½" square, from each print, for a total of 120.

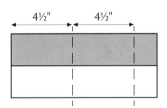

Cut 2 segments
from each strip set.

3 Sew two matching segments into a block as shown. Make a total of 60 blocks that measure 4½" × 8½", including seam allowances.

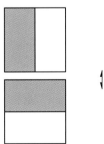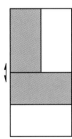

Make 60 blocks,
4½" x 8½".

Assembling the Quilt Top

1 Arrange 10 blocks into a row, rotating the blocks as shown and alternating the gray and black prints as desired. You may want to lay out all the rows before joining the blocks, to make sure you like the placement of the fabrics. Make six rows that measure 8½" × 40½", including seam allowances.

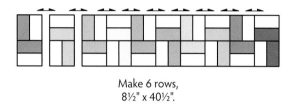

Make 6 rows,
8½" x 40½".

2 Referring to the quilt assembly diagram at right, arrange and sew the rows together. The quilt top should measure 40½" × 48½", including seam allowances.

Adding the Border

1 Piece the five gray 4½" × 42" strips together end to end. From this length, cut two strips, 48½" long, and sew them to the sides of the quilt top.

2 From the remainder of the gray strip, cut two strips, 48½" long, and sew them to the top and bottom of the quilt top. The completed quilt top should measure 48½" × 56½".

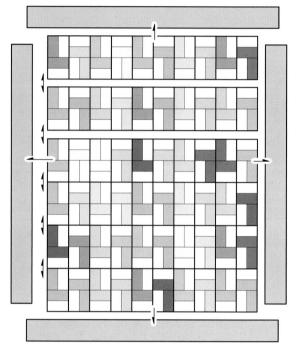

Quilt assembly

Finishing

If you need more information on any of the finishing steps, go to ShopMartingale.com/HowtoQuilt for free downloadable instructions.

1 Layer the backing, batting, and quilt top; baste the layers together. Hand or machine quilt as desired. Our quilt was quilted with narrow petals in the print areas, teardrop shapes in the white background, and a feather pattern in the border.

2 Trim and square up the quilt. Make the binding using the black 2¼"-wide strips and attach it to the quilt.

Positive and Negative

Finished quilt: 68" × 68" • Finished block: 9½" × 9½"

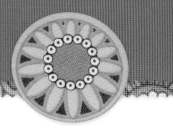

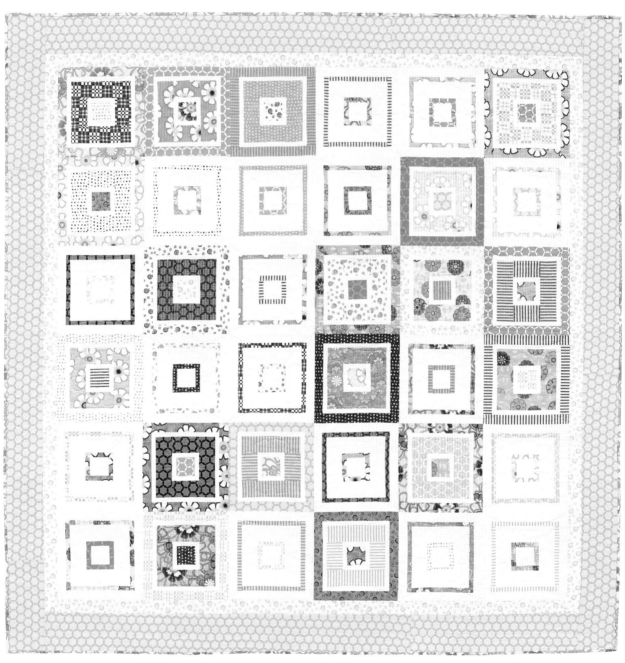

Made with the Good Morning fabric line by Me and My Sister Designs

This quilt is one of our favorites. Simply placing stronger fabrics in different positions within the block causes some blocks to rise to the surface and others to sink into the background. "Baking" with Layer Cake squares can be so much fun!

Materials

Yardage is based on 42"-wide fabric.

36 squares, 10" × 10", of assorted prints for blocks*
2⅓ yards of white solid for blocks
½ yard of light green print for inner border
1 yard of medium green print for outer border
⅝ yard of blue print for binding
4¼ yards of fabric for backing
76" × 76" piece of batting

A Moda Layer Cake contains 42 squares, 10" × 10".

Cutting

All measurements include ¼" seam allowances. Divide the 36 squares into 2 sets of 18 squares each. Refer to "Cutting and Sorting Guide" on page 17 when cutting the 10" squares.

From each of the 18 squares from set 1, cut:
2 rectangles, 1½" × 10" (36 total)
2 rectangles, 1½" × 8" (36 total)
2 rectangles, 1" × 3½" (36 total)
2 rectangles, 1" × 2½" (36 total)
1 square, 2½" × 2½" (18 total)

From each of the 18 squares from set 2, cut:
2 rectangles, 1" × 8" (36 total)
2 rectangles, 1" × 7" (36 total)
2 rectangles, 2¼" × 7" (36 total)
2 rectangles, 2¼" × 3½" (36 total)

From the white solid, cut:
17 strips, 1½" × 42"; crosscut into:
  • 36 rectangles, 1½" × 8"
  • 36 rectangles, 1½" × 10"
11 strips, 2¼" × 42"; crosscut into:
  • 36 rectangles, 2¼" × 3½"
  • 36 rectangles, 2¼" × 7"
2 strips, 2½" × 42"; crosscut into 18 squares, 2½" × 2½"
21 strips, 1" × 42"; crosscut into:
  • 36 rectangles, 1" × 2½"
  • 36 rectangles, 1" × 3½"
  • 36 rectangles, 1" × 7"
  • 36 rectangles, 1" × 8"

From the light green print, cut:
6 strips, 2" × 42"

From the medium green print, cut:
7 strips, 4¼" × 42"

From the blue print, cut:
8 strips, 2¼" × 42"

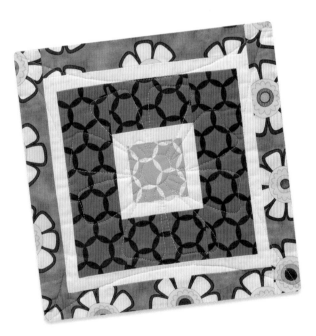

Cutting and Sorting Guide

Refer to these diagrams when cutting the 10" squares and sort the pieces as directed.

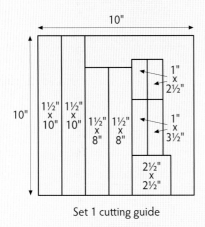

Set 1 cutting guide

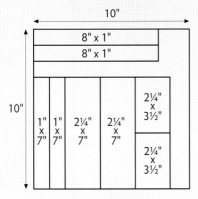

Set 2 cutting guide

1 Pin together and set aside groups of matching prints as follows:

- 2 rectangles, 1½" × 8", and 2 rectangles, 1½" × 10"
- 2 rectangles, 1" × 2½", and 2 rectangles, 1" × 3½"

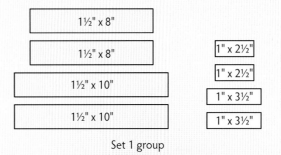

Set 1 group

2 Set aside the 2½" squares. They do not need to be sorted or pinned into any groups.

3 Pin together and set aside groups of matching prints as follows:

- 2 rectangles, 1" × 7", and 2 rectangles, 1" × 8"
- 2 rectangles, 2¼" × 3½", and 2 rectangles, 2¼" × 7"

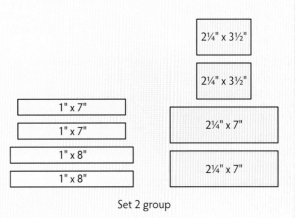

Set 2 group

Making the Blocks

Use a ¼"-wide seam allowance and a small stitch length throughout. Press all seam allowances open, unless otherwise noted.

BLOCK A

1 Using a pinned-together group, sew two print 1" × 2½" rectangles to opposite sides of a white 2½" square. Then sew two print 1" × 3½" rectangles to the top and bottom as shown.

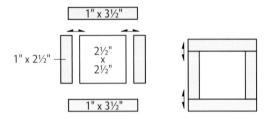

2 Sew two white 2¼" × 3½" rectangles to opposite sides of the unit. Then sew two white 2¼" × 7" rectangles to the top and bottom.

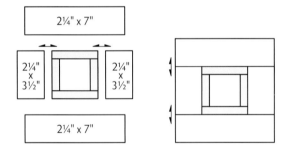

3 Using a pinned-together group, sew two print 1" × 7" rectangles to the sides of the unit. Then sew two print 1" × 8" rectangles to the top and bottom.

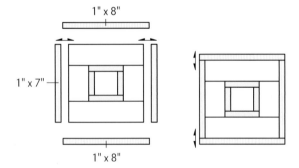

4 Sew two white 1½" × 8" rectangles to the sides of the unit. Then sew two white 1½" × 10" rectangles to the top and bottom to complete block A. Make a total of 18 A blocks that measure 10" square, including seam allowances.

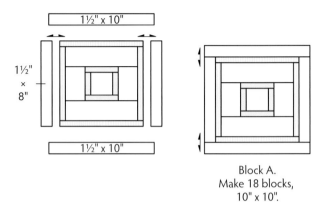

Block A.
Make 18 blocks,
10" x 10".

BLOCK B

1 Sew two white 1" × 2½" rectangles to opposite sides of a print 2½" square. Then sew two white 1" × 3½" rectangles to the top and bottom.

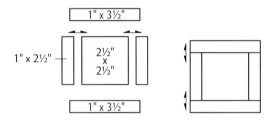

2 Using a pinned-together group, sew two print 2¼" × 3½" rectangles to the sides of the unit. Then sew two print 2¼" × 7" rectangles to the top and bottom.

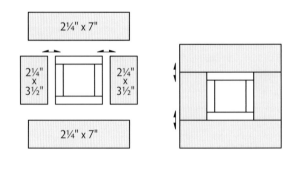

3 Sew two white 1" × 7" rectangles to the sides of the unit. Then sew two white 1" × 8" rectangles to the top and bottom.

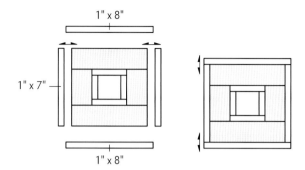

4 Using a pinned-together group, sew two print 1½" × 8" rectangles to the sides of the unit. Then sew two print 1½" × 10" rectangles to the top and bottom to complete block B. Make a total of 18 B blocks that measure 10" square, including seam allowances.

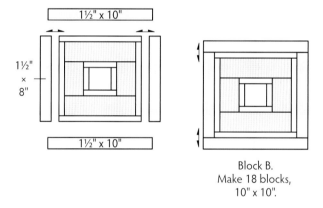

Block B.
Make 18 blocks,
10" x 10".

Assembling the Quilt Top

Referring to the quilt assembly diagram at right, arrange the blocks in six rows of six blocks each. Sew the blocks in each row together, and then join the rows. The quilt top should measure 57½" square, including seam allowances.

Adding Borders

1 For the inner border, piece the six light green 2" × 42" strips together end to end. From this length, cut two strips, 57½" long, and sew them to the sides of the quilt top.

2 From the remainder of the light green strip, cut two strips, 60½" long, and sew them to the top and bottom of the quilt top. The quilt top should now measure 60½" square, including seam allowances.

3 For the outer border, piece the seven medium green 4¼" × 42" strips together end to end. From this length, cut two strips, 60½" long, and sew them to the sides of the quilt top.

4 From the remainder of the medium green strip, cut two strips, 68" long, and sew them to the top and bottom of the quilt top. The completed quilt top should measure 68" square.

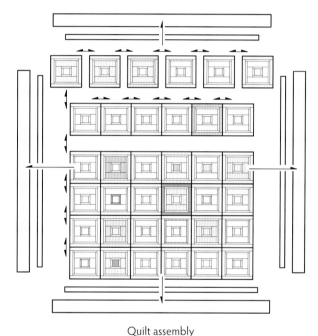

Quilt assembly

Finishing

If you need more information on any of the finishing steps, go to ShopMartingale.com/HowtoQuilt for free downloadable instructions.

1 Layer the backing, batting, and quilt top; baste the layers together. Hand or machine quilt as desired. Our quilt features floral designs within the blocks and feathers and loops in the border.

2 Trim and square up the quilt. Make the binding using the blue 2¼"-wide strips and attach it to the quilt.

Flower Power

Finished quilt: 59½" × 71" • Finished block: 10" × 10"

Made with the Hi De Ho fabric line by Me and My Sister Designs

We love flowers on cakes—the more of those big globs of frosting blossoms, the better! Here we've turned the tables and made zero-calorie fabric flowers out of a Layer Cake. This quilt is much easier to piece than it looks. Just follow the step-by-step "recipe."

Materials

Yardage is based on 42"-wide fabric.

30 squares, 10" × 10", of assorted prints for blocks*
5¼ yards of white solid for blocks, sashing, and border
⅛ yard of yellow solid for block centers
⅝ yard of multicolored stripe for binding
4 yards of fabric for backing
68" × 79" piece of batting

A Moda Layer Cake contains 42 squares, 10" × 10".

Cutting

All measurements include¼" seam allowances.

From *each* of the print 10" squares, cut:
1 rectangle, 7½" × 8½" (30 total)

From the white solid, cut:
8 strips, 10" × 42"; crosscut into 30 squares, 10" × 10". Cut the squares in half diagonally to yield 60 triangles.
6 strips, 7½" × 42"; crosscut into 60 rectangles, 3½" × 7½"
22 strips, 2" × 42"; crosscut 8 strips into 24 rectangles, 2" × 10½"

From the yellow solid, cut:
2 strips, 1¾" × 42"; crosscut into 30 squares, 1¾" × 1¾"

From the multicolored stripe, cut:
7 strips, 2¼" × 42"

Making the Blocks

Use a ¼"-wide seam allowance and a small stitch length throughout. Press all seam allowances open, unless otherwise noted.

1 Sew white 3½" × 7½" rectangles to opposite sides of a print 7½" × 8½" rectangle. Cut the unit as shown to yield four segments, 1¾" × 14½".

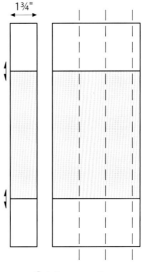

1¾"

Cut 4 segments.

2 Mark the center of one segment by folding in half and finger pressing to make a crease. Fold two triangles in half and finger press to mark the center of the diagonal. Center and sew one segment from step 1 between the two white triangles as shown. Cut the unit in half diagonally.

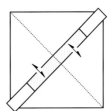 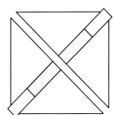

3 Mark the center of a second segment from step 1 and the triangles by folding and finger pressing. Center and sew the second segment between the two triangles. Cut this unit in half horizontally.

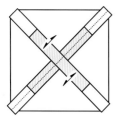
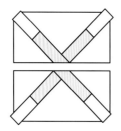

4 Mark the center of a third segment from step 1 and the rectangle units by folding and finger pressing. Center and sew the third segment between the two halves. Cut this unit in half vertically.

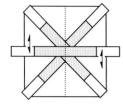
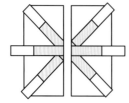

5 Cut the last segment from step 1 in half and sew a yellow 1¾" square between the two halves.

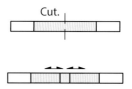

Cut.

6 Center and sew the step 5 unit between the two halves from step 4. Keeping the yellow square centered, trim the block to measure 10½" square, including seam allowances. Make a total of 30 blocks.

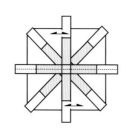
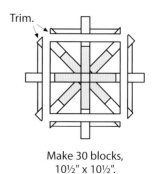

Trim.

Make 30 blocks,
10½" x 10½".

Adding the Border

1 Piece the remaining seven white 2" × 42" strips together end to end. From this length, cut two strips, 68" long, and sew them to the sides of the quilt top.

2 From the remainder of the white strip, cut two strips, 59½" long, and sew them to the top and bottom of the quilt top. The completed quilt top should measure 59½" × 71".

Quilt assembly

Finishing

If you need more information on any of the finishing steps, go to ShopMartingale.com/HowtoQuilt for free downloadable instructions.

1 Layer the backing, batting, and quilt top; baste the layers together. Hand or machine quilt as desired. Our quilt features an overall pattern of spirals set against a background that resembles pebbles.

2 Trim and square up the quilt. Make the binding using the multicolored stripe 2¼"-wide strips and attach it to the quilt.

Assembling the Quilt Top

1 Arrange and sew five Flower blocks and four white 2" × 10½" sashing rectangles into a row. Make six rows that measure 10½" × 56½", including seam allowances.

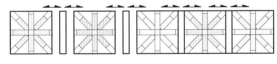

Make 6 rows,
10½" x 56½".

2 Piece seven of the white 2" × 42" strips together end to end. From this length, cut five strips, 56½" long, for sashing.

3 Arrange and sew the six block rows and five white sashing strips together in alternating positions. The quilt top should measure 56½" × 68", including seam allowances.

Beanstalk

Made with the Weeds fabric line by Me and My Sister Designs

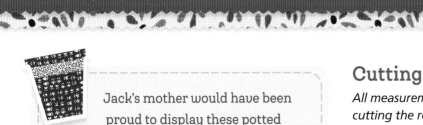

Jack's mother would have been proud to display these potted beauties in her yard. The pots are a snap to make, and the leaves are too—almost like magic! If you're in a hurry, try a row all by itself as a table runner or as a banner for your door.

Materials

Yardage is based on 42"-wide fabric.

24 squares, 10" × 10", of assorted black, gray, and red prints for Leaf blocks*

7 squares, 10" × 10", of assorted red prints for Pot blocks*

2½ yards of white print for blocks, sashing, and border

⅜ yard of black tone on tone for Leaf blocks

⅝ yard of gray solid for binding

3¼ yards of fabric for backing

57" × 75" piece of batting

A Moda Layer Cake contains 42 squares, 10" × 10".

Cutting

All measurements include ¼" seam allowances. When cutting the red 10" squares for the pots, keep like prints together.

From 6 of the red 10" squares for Pot blocks, cut:
1 rectangle, 1½" × 6½" (6 total)
1 rectangle, 4½" × 6½" (6 total)

From the remaining red 10" square for Pot blocks, cut:
6 rectangles, 1½" × 6½" (for pot bands)

From the white print, cut:
5 strips, 2" × 42"; crosscut into 96 squares, 2" × 2"
10 strips, 3" × 42"; crosscut into 96 rectangles, 3" × 4"
16 strips, 2½" × 42"; crosscut 2 strips into 12 rectangles, 2½" × 6½"

From *each* of the print 10" squares for Leaf blocks, cut:
4 squares, 4" × 4" (96 total)

From the black tone on tone, cut:
5 strips, 2" × 42"; crosscut into 96 squares, 2" × 2"

From the gray solid, cut:
7 strips, 2¼" × 42"

Making the Blocks

Use a ¼"-wide seam allowance and a small stitch length throughout. Press all seam allowances open, unless otherwise noted.

POT BLOCKS

For each block, select the following:

- 1 red rectangle, 1½" × 6½", and 1 matching red rectangle, 4½" × 6½"
- 1 red rectangle, 1½" × 6½", for pot band
- 2 white rectangles, 2½" × 6½"

1 Sew the red 1½" × 6½" rectangle for the pot band to the top of the red 4½" × 6½" rectangle.

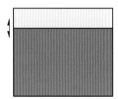

2 Measure in ¼" from each side at the top of the pot unit and make a pencil mark. Measure in 1¼" from each side at the bottom of the pot unit and make a pencil mark. Draw a line between the top and bottom marks on each side, and cut on the drawn lines.

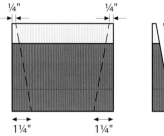
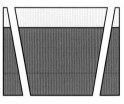

3 Sew a white 2½" × 6½" rectangle to each side of the pot.

4 Mark the center of the matching red 1½" × 6½" rectangle by folding in half and finger pressing a crease. Mark the center of the pot unit by folding and finger pressing. Center the rectangle along the top of the pot unit, aligning the creases. Sew across the entire unit as shown and press.

5 Trim the block to measure 6½" square, including seam allowances. Make six Pot blocks.

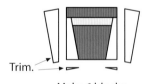

Trim.

Make 6 blocks,
6½" x 6½".

LEAF BLOCKS

For each block, select the following:

- 1 black, gray, or red square, 4" × 4"
- 1 black tone-on-tone square, 2" × 2"
- 1 white square, 2" × 2", and 1 white rectangle, 3" × 4"

1 Draw a diagonal line from corner to corner on the wrong side of each black tone-on-tone 2" square and each white 2" square. A chalk pen or pencil works well on dark fabrics.

2 With right sides together, position a marked black square and a marked white square on opposite corners of a black, gray, or red 4" square. Stitch on the marked lines. Trim the seam allowances to ¼". Flip and press. Make 96 leaf units.

Make 96.

3 Sew a white 3" × 4" rectangle to the left side of 48 leaf units and to the right side of the remaining 48 leaf units to make a total of 96 Leaf blocks. The blocks should measure 6½" × 4".

Make 48 of each block, 6½" x 4".

Assembling the Quilt Top

1 Referring to the diagram above right, sew 16 Leaf blocks and one Pot block into a vertical column. Make six columns, noting that—just as in nature—the leaf direction doesn't alternate in a uniform manner. Each column should measure 6½" × 62½", including seam allowances. Press the seam allowances open.

2 Piece eight of the white 2½" × 42" strips together end to end. From this length, cut five strips, 62½" long, for sashing.

3 Arrange and sew the six columns and five sashing strips together in alternating positions. The quilt top should now measure 46½" × 62½".

Adding the Border

1 Piece the remaining six white 2½" × 42" strips together end to end. From this length, cut two strips, 62½" long, and sew them to the sides of the quilt top.

2 From the remainder of the white strip, cut two strips, 50½" long, and sew them to the top and bottom of the quilt top. The completed quilt top should measure 50½" × 66½".

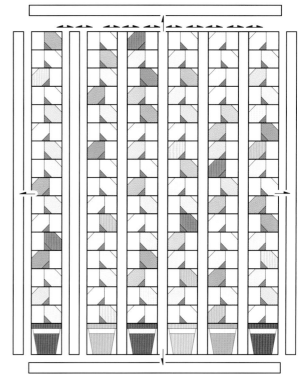

Quilt assembly

Finishing

If you need more information on any of the finishing steps, go to ShopMartingale.com/HowtoQuilt for free downloadable instructions.

1 Layer the backing, batting, and quilt top; baste the layers together. Hand or machine quilt as desired. Our quilt includes arcs within the Leaf blocks and a vine of curling leaves between the beanstalks.

2 Trim and square up the quilt. Make the binding using the gray solid 2¼"-wide strips and attach it to the quilt.

Made with the Sun Drops fabric line by Corey Yoder

Look at all the fun layers in this quilt! This recipe offers the perfect opportunity to show off a Layer Cake as well as your skills as a baker. Time to round up your ingredients, slice up that Layer Cake, and serve it with style.

Materials

Yardage is based on 42"-wide fabric.

25 squares, 10" × 10", of assorted prints for blocks*
2⅛ yards of white solid for blocks
⅝ yard of orange print for binding
3½ yards of fabric for backing
63" × 63" piece of batting

A Moda Layer Cake contains 42 squares, 10" × 10".

Cutting

All measurements include ¼" seam allowances.

From the white solid, cut:
7 strips, 10" × 42"; crosscut into 25 squares, 10" × 10"

From the orange print, cut:
6 strips, 2¼" × 42"

Making the Blocks

Use a ¼"-wide seam allowance and a small stitch length throughout. Press all seam allowances open, unless otherwise noted.

Divide the 25 print squares into five stacks of five squares each. Each stack will be cut and sewn in a different manner to make the blocks.

STACK 1

1 Layer one print 10" square and one white 10" square together with right sides facing up. Make three cuts as shown to yield the following pieces:

- 1 print and 1 white rectangle, 2½" × 10"
- 2 print and 2 white rectangles, 1½" × 10"
- 1 print and 1 white rectangle, 4½" × 10"

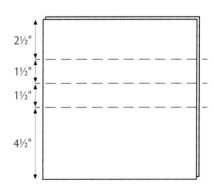

2 Arrange and sew the rectangles into two blocks as shown.

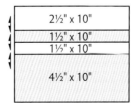

Stack 1

3 Trim the blocks to measure 8½" square, including seam allowances.

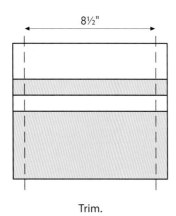

8½"

Trim.

4 Repeat steps 1–3 with the remaining four prints to make 10 of these stack 1 blocks.

STACK 2

1 Layer one print 10" square and one white 10" square together with right sides facing up. Make three cuts as shown to yield the following pieces:

- 1 print and 1 white rectangle, 2" × 10"
- 1 print and 1 white rectangle, 3" × 10"
- 1 print and 1 white rectangle, 1½" × 10"
- 1 print and 1 white rectangle, 3½" × 10"

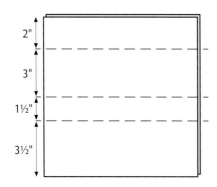

2"

3"

1½"

3½"

2 Arrange and sew the rectangles into two blocks as shown.

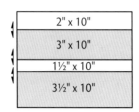

2" x 10"		2" x 10"
3" x 10"		3" x 10"
1½" x 10"		1½" x 10"
3½" x 10"		3½" x 10"

Stack 2

3 Trim the blocks to measure 8½" square, including seam allowances.

4 Repeat steps 1–3 with the remaining four prints to make 10 of these stack 2 blocks.

STACK 3

1 Layer one print 10" square and one white 10" square together with right sides facing up. Make three cuts as shown to yield the following pieces:

- 2 print and 2 white rectangles, 1½" × 10"
- 1 print and 1 white rectangle, 3" × 10"
- 1 print and 1 white rectangle, 4" × 10"

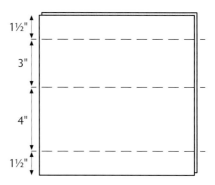

1½"

3"

4"

1½"

2 Arrange and sew the rectangles into two blocks as shown.

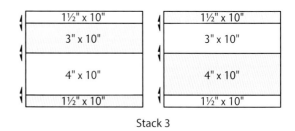

1½" x 10"		1½" x 10"
3" x 10"		3" x 10"
4" x 10"		4" x 10"
1½" x 10"		1½" x 10"

Stack 3

3 Trim the blocks to measure 8½" square, including seam allowances.

4 Repeat steps 1–3 with the remaining four prints to make 10 of these stack 3 blocks.

STACK 4

1 Layer one print 10" square and one white 10" square together with right sides facing up. Make three cuts as shown to yield the following pieces:

- 3 print and 3 white rectangles, 1½" × 10"
- 1 print and 1 white rectangle, 5½" × 10"

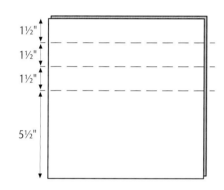

2 Arrange and sew the rectangles into two blocks as shown.

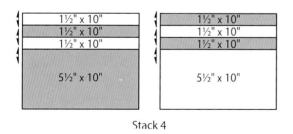

Stack 4

3 Trim the blocks to measure 8½" square, including seam allowances.

4 Repeat steps 1–3 with the remaining four prints to make 10 of these stack 4 blocks.

STACK 5

1 Layer one print 10" square and one white 10" square together with right sides facing up. Make three cuts as shown to yield the following pieces:

- 2 print and 2 white rectangles, 1½" × 10"
- 1 white and 1 print rectangle, 3" × 10"
- 1 white and 1 print rectangle, 4" × 10"

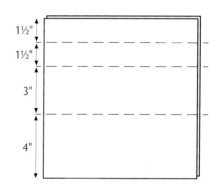

2 Arrange and sew the rectangles into two blocks as shown.

Stack 5

3 Trim the blocks to measure 8½" square, including seam allowances.

4 Repeat steps 1–3 with the remaining four prints to make 10 of these stack 5 blocks.

Assembling the Quilt Top

1 Referring to the quilt assembly diagram below, arrange the blocks in seven rows of seven blocks each, rotating them as shown. (You'll have one block left over.) Sew the blocks in each row together. The rows should measure 8½" × 56½", including seam allowances.

2 Sew the rows together. The quilt top should measure 56½" square.

Finishing

If you need more information on any of the finishing steps, go to ShopMartingale.com/HowtoQuilt for free downloadable instructions.

1 Layer the backing, batting, and quilt top; baste the layers together. Hand or machine quilt as desired. Our quilt includes a diagonal grid, with flowers quilted inside the grid.

2 Trim and square up the quilt. Make the binding using the orange 2¼"-wide strips and attach it to the quilt.

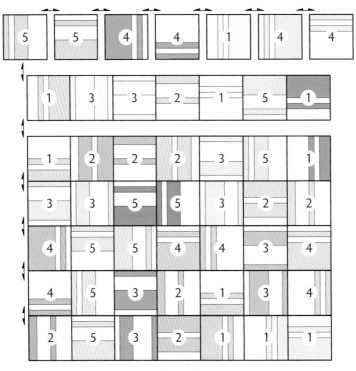

Quilt assembly

Rain Chain

Finished quilt: 78½" × 80½" • **Finished block: 14" × 9"**

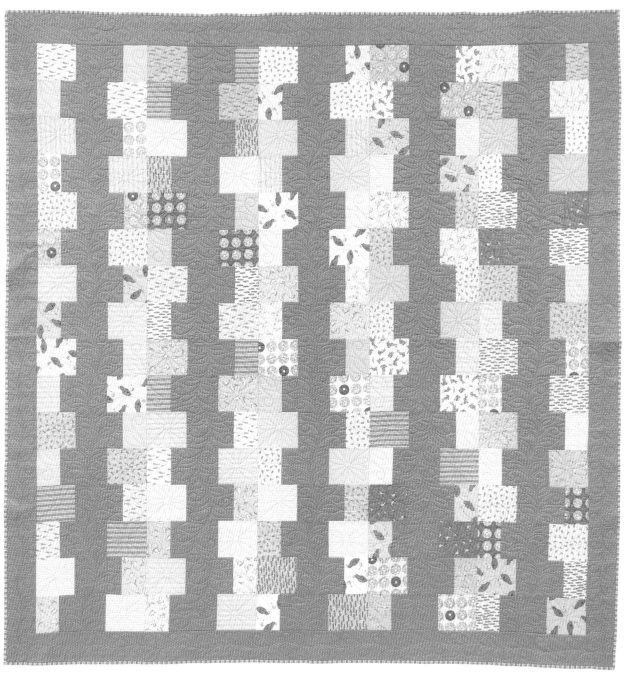

Made with the Darling Dickens fabric line by Lydia Nelson

Can't you just imagine a cascade of gentle rain streaming down the sides of these rows of offset blocks? This would be an ideal project for a rainy day, or a sunny day for that matter! It's a super fast, fun, and easy way to finally use that favorite Layer Cake you've been hoarding.

Materials

Yardage is based on 42"-wide fabric.

40 squares, 10" × 10", of assorted prints for blocks*
3¼ yards of tan dot for blocks and border
⅔ yard of tan stripe for binding
7½ yards of fabric for backing
87" × 89" piece of batting

A Moda Layer Cake contains 42 squares, 10" × 10".

Cutting

All measurements include ¼" seam allowances.

From *each* of the print 10" squares, cut:
1 rectangle, 3½" × 10" (40 total)
1 rectangle, 5½" × 10" (40 total)

From the tan dot, cut:
7 strips, 10" × 42"; crosscut into 40 rectangles,
    6½" × 10"
8 strips, 4½" × 42"

From the tan stripe, cut:
9 strips, 2¼" × 42"

Making the Blocks

Use a ¼"-wide seam allowance and a small stitch length throughout. Press all seam allowances open, unless otherwise noted.

1 Sew a print 3½" × 10" rectangle and a coordinating print 5½" × 10" rectangle to the long edges of a tan dot 6½" × 10" rectangle to make a strip set. Cut the strip set in half to yield two segments, 5" × 14½".

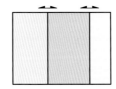
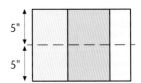

2 Rotate one segment, and then sew the segments back together as shown to make a block that measures 14½" × 9½", including seam allowances. Make a total of 40 blocks, with the larger squares always in the upper-left and lower-right corners.

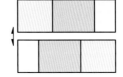
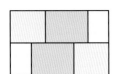

Make 40 units,
14½" x 9½".

Assembling the Quilt Top

1 Referring to the quilt assembly diagram below, arrange the blocks into five vertical rows of eight blocks each. Sew the blocks in each row together. The rows should measure 14½" × 72½".

2 Sew the rows together. The quilt top should now measure 70½" × 72½", including seam allowances.

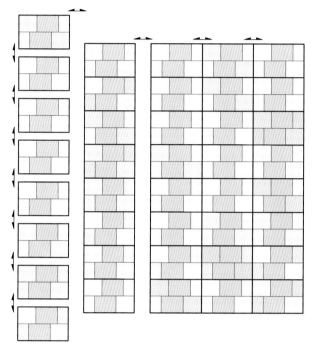

Quilt assembly

Adding the Border

1 Piece the eight tan dot 4½" × 42" strips together end to end. From this length, cut two strips, 72½" long, and sew them to the sides of the quilt top.

2 From the remainder of the tan dot strip, cut two strips, 78½" long, and sew them to the top and bottom of the quilt top. The completed quilt top should measure 78½" × 80½".

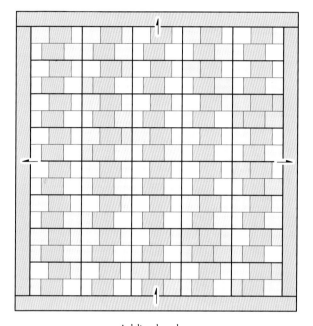

Adding borders

Finishing

If you need more information on any of the finishing steps, go to ShopMartingale.com/HowtoQuilt for free downloadable instructions.

1 Layer the backing, batting, and quilt top; baste the layers together. Hand or machine quilt as desired. Our quilt has long curving vines of pointed leaves alternating with spiral tendrils. The squares feature a quilted daisy.

2 Trim and square up the quilt. Make the binding using the tan stripe 2¼"-wide strips and attach it to the quilt.

Off the Grid

Made with the Olive's Flower Market fabric line by Lella Boutique

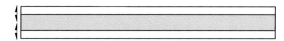

Here's a quilt recipe to really immortalize a favorite Layer Cake. You'll keep much of the print intact with these blocks, and of course, you can arrange them in many different ways. Stay on the path and follow the simple instructions to turn fabulous fabrics into a fabulous quilt!

Materials

Yardage is based on 42"-wide fabric.

25 squares, 10" × 10", of assorted prints for blocks*
⅝ yard of black dot for blocks
1½ yards of white print for blocks and border
½ yard of black print for binding
3½ yards of fabric for backing
60" × 60" piece of batting

A Moda Layer Cake contains 42 squares, 10" × 10".

Cutting

All measurements include ¼" seam allowances.

From each of the print 10" squares, cut:
2 triangles* (50 total)

From the black dot, cut:
1 strip, 17" × 42"; crosscut into 25 strips, 1½" × 17"

From the white print, cut:
2 strips, 17" × 42"; crosscut into 50 strips, 1" × 17"
6 strips, 2¼" × 42"

From the black print, cut:
6 strips, 2¼" × 42"

Cut each square in half diagonally; keep like prints together.

Making the Blocks

Use a ¼"-wide seam allowance and a small stitch length throughout. Press all seam allowances open, unless otherwise noted.

1 Sew a white 1" × 17" strip to each long edge of a black dot 1½" × 17" strip. Make 25 strip sets.

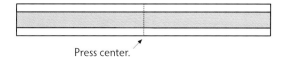

Make 25.

2 Mark the center of each strip set by folding it in half and finger-pressing or lightly tapping the center with a warm iron. In the same manner, fold each print triangle in half and mark the center of the long diagonal edge.

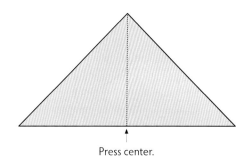

Press center.

Press center.

3 Arrange and sew a strip set between two matching triangles, aligning the center points. Make 25.

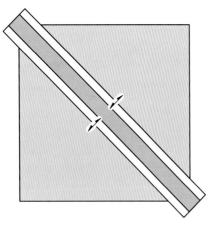

Make 25.

4 Trim the blocks to measure 10½" square, including seam allowances.

Trim.

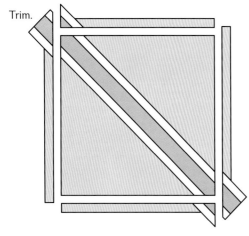

Make 25 blocks,
10½" x 10½".

Assembling the Quilt Top

1 Referring to the quilt assembly diagram above right, arrange the blocks into five rows of five blocks each, rotating them as shown. Sew the blocks in each row together. The rows should measure 10½" × 50½", including seam allowances.

2 Sew the rows together. The quilt top should now measure 50½" square, including seam allowances.

Adding the Border

1 Piece the six white 2¼" × 42" strips together end to end. From this length, cut two strips, 50½" long, and sew them to the sides of the quilt top.

2 From the remainder of the white strip, cut two strips, 54" long, and sew them to the top and bottom of the quilt top. The completed quilt top should measure 54" square.

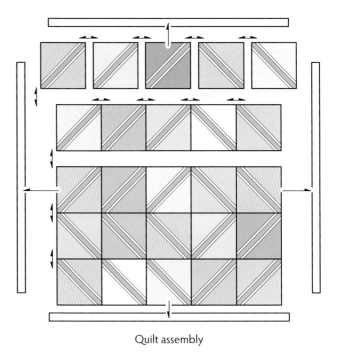

Quilt assembly

Finishing

If you need more information on any of the finishing steps, go to ShopMartingale.com/HowtoQuilt for free downloadable instructions.

1 Layer the backing, batting, and quilt top; baste the layers together. Hand or machine quilt as desired. Our quilt has alternating motifs of leafy vines and petal shapes in the diagonal areas. The border features a scallop design.

2 Trim and square up the quilt. Make the binding using the black print 2¼"-wide strips and attach it to the quilt.

Cakewalk

Finished quilt: 64½" × 64½" • Finished block: 8" × 8"

Made with the Handmade fabric line by Bonnie and Camille

Hey, we had to have at least one quilt in this book with the word *cake* in the title! Here you have it–think of the block centers as the squares in the path of a cakewalk. Buy a ticket, step on a square, and walk until the music stops. Whoever is standing on the winning square wins the cake!

Materials

Yardage is based on 42"-wide fabric.

36 squares, 10" × 10", of assorted prints for blocks*
1¼ yards of white solid for blocks and inner border
2 yards of turquoise print for outer border**
⅝ yard of red print for binding
4⅛ yards of fabric for backing
73" × 73" piece of batting

A Moda Layer Cake contains 42 squares, 10" × 10".

**The outer-border fabric shown was cut on the lengthwise grain. If you wish to cut the borders crosswise and piece strips together, you'll need just 1¼ yards.*

Cutting

All measurements include¼" seam allowances.

From each of the print 10" squares, cut:
4 squares, 4½" × 4½" (144 total)*

From the white solid, cut:
9 strips, 2½" × 42"; crosscut into 144 squares,
    2½" × 2½"
6 strips, 2½" × 42"

From the turquoise print, cut:
6 strips, 6½" × 42"

From the red print, cut:
7 strips, 2¼" × 42"

**Keep like prints together.*

Making the Blocks

Use a ¼"-wide seam allowance and a small stitch length throughout. Press all seam allowances open, unless otherwise noted.

1 Draw a diagonal line on the wrong side of each white 2½" square. With right sides together, place a marked square on one corner of each print 4½" square as shown. Stitch on the marked line. Trim the seam allowance to ¼", flip, and press. Make 144 units.

Make 144 units.

2 Arrange and sew four matching units together as shown. The block should measure 8½" square, including seam allowances. Make a total of 36 blocks.

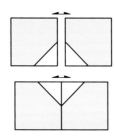 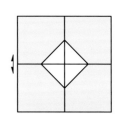

Make 36 blocks,
8½" x 8½".

Assembling the Quilt Top

1 Referring to the quilt assembly diagram at right, arrange the blocks in six rows of six blocks each. Sew the blocks in each row together.

2 Sew the rows together. The quilt top should now measure 48½" square, including seam allowances.

Adding Borders

1 For the inner border, piece the six white 2½" × 42" strips together end to end. From this length, cut two strips, 48½" long, and sew them to the sides of the quilt top.

2 From the remainder of the white strip, cut two strips, 52½" long, and sew them to the top and bottom of the quilt top. The quilt top should now measure 52½" square, including seam allowances.

3 For the outer border, piece the six turquoise 6½" × 42" strips together end to end. From this length, cut two strips, 52½" long, and sew them to the sides of the quilt top.

4 From the remainder of the turquoise strip, cut two strips, 64½" long, and sew them to the top and bottom of the quilt top. The completed quilt top should measure 64½" square.

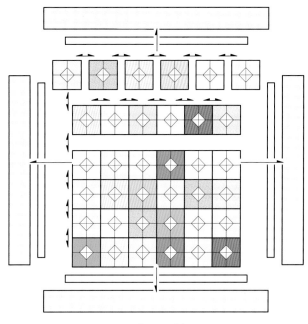

Quilt assembly

Finishing

If you need more information on any of the finishing steps, go to ShopMartingale.com/HowtoQuilt for free downloadable instructions.

1 Layer the backing, batting, and quilt top; baste the layers together. Hand or machine quilt as desired. Our quilt includes four hearts in the white squares surrounded by feathered wreath designs. The inner border is quilted with hearts and the outer border features a feathered vine.

2 Trim and square up the quilt. Make the binding using the red 2¼"-wide strips and attach it to the quilt.

Chevrons, Anyone?

Finished quilt: 60½" × 75½" • Finished block: 7½" × 7½"

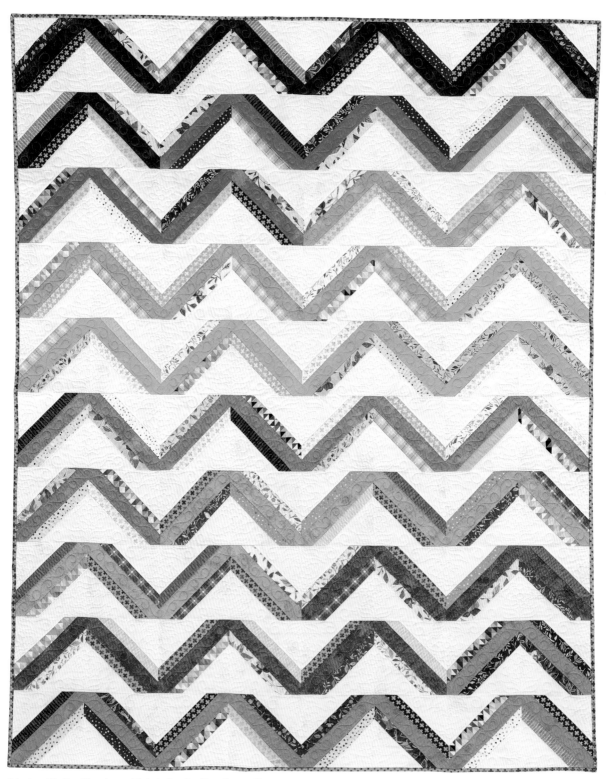

Made with the Hazelwood fabric line by One Canoe Two

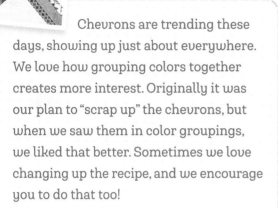

Chevrons are trending these days, showing up just about everywhere. We love how grouping colors together creates more interest. Originally it was our plan to "scrap up" the chevrons, but when we saw them in color groupings, we liked that better. Sometimes we love changing up the recipe, and we encourage you to do that too!

Materials

Yardage is based on 42"-wide fabric. Fat quarters measure 18" × 21".

40 squares, 10" × 10", of assorted prints for blocks*
8 fat quarters of coordinating solids for blocks
3 yards of white solid for blocks
⅝ yard of red print for binding
4¾ yards of fabric for backing
69" × 84" piece of batting

A Moda Layer Cake contains 42 squares, 10" × 10".

Cutting

All measurements include ¼" seam allowances.

From *each* of the print 10" squares, cut:
4 rectangles, 1½" × 10" (160 total)

From *each* of the solid fat quarters, cut:
1 strip, 12" × 21"; crosscut into 10 rectangles, 2" × 12" (80 total)

From the white solid, cut:
14 strips, 6½" × 42"; crosscut into 80 squares, 6½" × 6½". Cut the squares in half diagonally to yield 160 triangles.

From the red print, cut:
8 strips, 2¼" × 42"

Making the Blocks

Use a ¼"-wide seam allowance and a small stitch length throughout. Press all seam allowances open, unless otherwise noted.

1. Mark the center of each print and solid rectangle by folding in half and lightly pressing with a warm iron.

2. Arrange two print 1½" × 10" rectangles and one coordinating solid 2" × 12" rectangle as shown, aligning the marked centers. Sew together to make the block center.

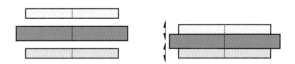

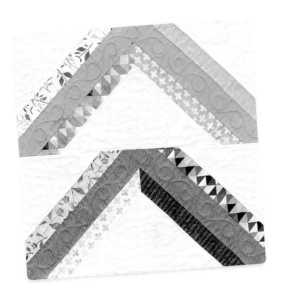

3 Gently fold two white triangles in half and lightly press with a warm iron to mark the center.

4 Sew a white triangle to each side of the block center, aligning the center creases. Trim the block to measure 8" square, including seam allowances. Make a total of 80 blocks.

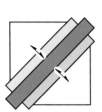 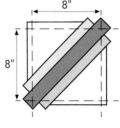

Make 80 blocks,
8" x 8".

Assembling the Quilt Top

1 Arrange eight blocks into a row, rotating the blocks as shown. Sew the blocks together. Make 10 rows that measure 8" × 60½", including seam allowances.

Make 10 rows,
8" x 60½".

2 Arrange and sew the rows together as shown. The completed quilt top should measure 60½" × 75½".

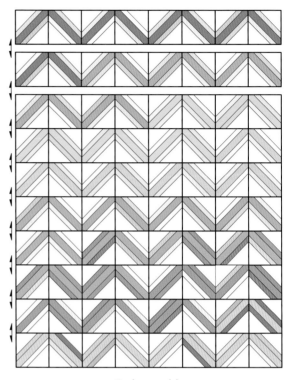

Quilt assembly

Finishing

If you need more information on any of the finishing steps, go to ShopMartingale.com/HowtoQuilt for free downloadable instructions.

1 Layer the backing, batting, and quilt top; baste the layers together. Hand or machine quilt as desired. Our quilt was quilted with scrolls and loops in the print areas and flowers and leaves in the white background.

2 Trim and square up the quilt. Make the binding using the red 2¼"-wide strips and attach it to the quilt.

Squared Circles

Finished quilt: 56½" × 56½" • Finished block: 16" × 16"

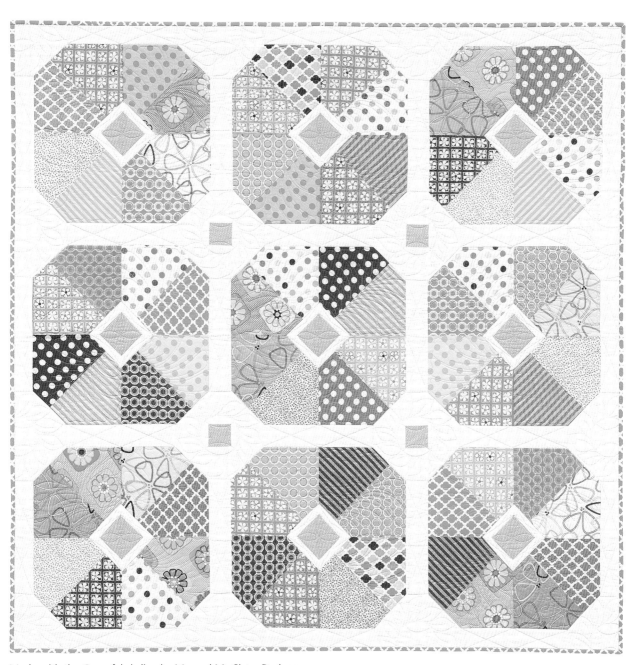

Made with the Grow fabric line by Me and My Sister Designs

When cutting a cake, Barb likes to cut the corners off first. Why, you ask? It's because the corners have the most frosting! Corners are crucial to this quilt, as well. You'll make the blocks simply by sewing squares to the corners and cutting them off. Grab a big glass of milk and have some quality time cutting and sewing this "cakey" sweet quilt.

Materials

Yardage is based on 42"-wide fabric.

36 squares, 10" × 10", of assorted prints for blocks*
1⅔ yards of white solid for blocks, sashing, and border
¼ yard of orange print for block centers and sashing squares
½ yard of turquoise print for binding
3⅝ yards of fabric for backing
63" × 63" piece of batting

A Moda Layer Cake contains 42 squares, 10" × 10".

Cutting

All measurements include ¼" seam allowances.

From *each* of the print 10" squares, cut:
2 triangles* (72 total)

From the white solid, cut:
7 strips, 3½" × 42"; crosscut into 72 squares, 3½" × 3½"

12 strips, 2½" × 42"; crosscut 6 strips into 12 strips, 2½" × 16½"

From the orange print, cut:
3 strips, 2½" × 42"; crosscut into 40 squares, 2½" × 2½"

From the turquoise print, cut:
6 strips, 2¼" × 42"

Cut each square in half diagonally.

Making the Blocks

Use a ¼"-wide seam allowance and a small stitch length throughout. Press all seam allowances open, unless otherwise noted.

For each block, select the following:

- 8 print triangles
- 8 white 3½" squares
- 4 orange 2½" squares

1 With right sides facing, sew two triangles together to make a half-square-triangle unit. Make four and trim the units to 8½" square, including seam allowances.

Make 4 units, 8½" x 8½".

2 Draw a diagonal line from corner to corner on the wrong side of eight white 3½" squares. Place marked white squares right sides together on opposite corners of each half-square-triangle unit. Stitch on the marked lines. Trim seam allowances to ¼" and press. Make four.

Make 4.

3 Draw a diagonal line from corner to corner on the wrong side of four orange 2½" squares. Repeat step 3 to sew a marked square on *one* white corner of each unit. Make four.

Make 4.

4 Arrange and sew the four units into a block as shown. The block should measure 16½" square, including seam allowances. Make a total of nine blocks.

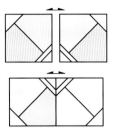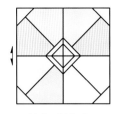

Make 9 blocks,
16½" x 16½".

Assembling the Quilt Top

1 Arrange and sew three blocks and two white 2½" × 16" sashing strips into a row. Make three rows that measure 16½" × 52½", including seam allowances.

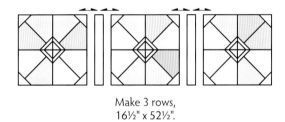

Make 3 rows,
16½" x 52½".

2 Sew three white 2½" × 16½" strips and two orange 2½" squares together to make a sashing row. Make two rows that measure 2½" × 52½", including seam allowances.

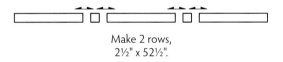

Make 2 rows,
2½" x 52½".

3 Sew the block and sashing rows together in alternating positions. The quilt top should now measure 52½" square, including seam allowances.

Adding the Border

1 Piece the six remaining white 2½" × 42" strips together end to end. From this length, cut two strips, 52½" long, and sew them to the sides of the quilt top.

2 From the remainder of the white strip, cut two strips, 56½" long, and sew them to the top and bottom of the quilt top. The completed quilt top should measure 56½" square.

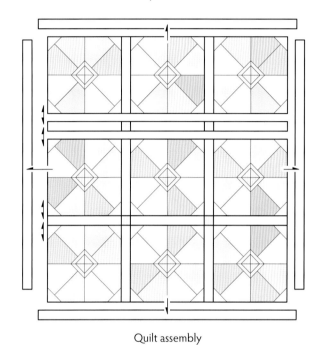

Quilt assembly

Finishing

If you need more information on any of the finishing steps, go to ShopMartingale.com/HowtoQuilt for free downloadable instructions.

1 Layer the backing, batting, and quilt top; baste the layers together. Hand or machine quilt as desired. Our quilt has petals in the block centers and feathers in the print sections of each block. Between the blocks are straight lines that create an X and wreaths of leaves.

2 Trim and square up the quilt. Make the binding using the turquoise 2¼"-wide strips and attach it to the quilt.

About the Authors

Acknowledgments

The very talented Sharon Elsberry, who runs her own business called Akamai Quilts, machine quilted all 11 quilts in this book. Her designs have really brought our quilts to life.

Sisters Barbara Groves and Mary Jacobson make up the popular design team of Me and My Sister Designs, based in Tempe, Arizona. Their belief in fast, fun, and easy designs can be seen in the quilts created for their pattern company, in their books, and in their fabric designs for Moda. To learn more, visit them at meandmysisterdesigns.com.